Hacking Fashion: Denim

CHERRY LAKE PUBLISHING • ANN ARBOR, MICHIGAN

by Kristin Fontichiaro

A Note to Adults: Please review the instructions for the activities in this book before allowing children to do them. Be sure to help them with any activities you do not think they can safely complete on their own.

A Note to Kids: Be sure to ask an adult for help with these activities when you need it. Always put your safety first!

Published in the United States of America by Cherry Lake Publishing
Ann Arbor, Michigan
www.cherrylakepublishing.com

Series Editor: Kristin Fontichiaro
Photo Credits: Cover and pages 1, 4, 7, 10, 14, 16, 18, 21, 22, and 25, ©Kristin Fontichiaro; page 5, ©Bill McChesney/tinyurl.com/glqdxx9/CC-BY-2.0

Library of Congress Cataloging-in-Publication Data
Names: Fontichiaro, Kristin, author.
Title: Hacking fashion. Denim / by Kristin Fontichiaro.
Other titles: Denim | 21st century skills innovation library. Makers as innovators.
Description: Ann Arbor, Michigan : Cherry Lake Publishing, [2016] |
 Series: 21st century skills innovation library. Makers as innovators |
 Audience: Grades 4 to 6. | Includes bibliographical references and index.
Identifiers: LCCN 2016000454| ISBN 9781634714167 [lib. bdg.] |
 ISBN 9781634714327 [pbk.] | ISBN 9781634714242 [pdf] |
 ISBN 9781634714402 [ebook]
Subjects: LCSH: Clothing and dress—Remaking—Juvenile literature. |
 Denim—Juvenile literature.
Classification: LCC TT550 .F655 2016 | DDC 746.9/2—dc23
LC record available at http://lccn.loc.gov/2016000454

Cherry Lake Publishing would like to acknowledge the work of The Partnership for 21st Century Learning. Please visit www.p21.org for more information.

Printed in the United States of America
Corporate Graphics
July 2016

Contents

Chapter 1

Thrifting for Denim

Are you a fashion hacker? Do you want to shorten, dye, fringe, cut, or change clothes to make them your own? If so, this book is for you.

We live in the era of fast fashion. Clothes are cheaper and more **abundant** than ever before. On the one hand, this is great news. We have endless fashion choices at low prices. But there are disadvantages, too. Sometimes cheap clothes don't hold up well over time. Most of the clothes we wear are also made in

You can find tons of great clothes and materials at low prices by shopping at thrift stores.

Shopping at thrift stores is a great way to cut down on the amount of clothing that gets thrown away.

distant countries. This means natural resources such as gas and coal are used to transport the clothes halfway around the world to your local mall. Worse, much of the world's clothing is made in places where working conditions are poor. People work long hours for little pay.

Meanwhile, more new clothes mean more discarded clothes. Sometimes old clothes even end up at **landfills**. This adds to the huge amount of garbage we already have. It's better when people donate old clothes to their favorite charities. These groups then resell the clothes at low prices. The funds raised support causes such as homelessness reduction and medical research. These stores are known as thrift stores or charity shops.

Many fashion hackers shop at thrift stores because they are inexpensive. "Thrifting" also cuts down on the amount of new materials you need to buy for your projects. Perhaps best of all, thrifting gives you the joy of discovering something you didn't expect!

In this book, we'll convert thrifted denim dresses, jackets, and pants into new **accessories**, costumes, containers, and playthings. So let's go thrifting!

You can find local thrift shops by checking the phone book (libraries have them), asking friends, or searching online. Read the shops' Web sites and social media feeds to learn about upcoming sales. This will help you buy clothes to hack at the lowest prices. If you buy a one-dollar pair of jeans to try a new fashion hacking project and it doesn't work out, you've only lost a dollar. But if you buy a 15-dollar pair of jeans and it doesn't work out, that might be the end of your creation budget!

Experienced thrifters visit stores frequently and stock up over time. Be patient. It may take a few visits to create a stash of denim for your projects. Browse the men's, women's, and plus-size departments, even if they aren't your typical size. Bigger clothing means more fabric you can use. (Sometimes, clothes get hung in the wrong department, too!) Some thrift stores are the size of supermarkets, so don't shop if you are hungry, tired, or thirsty. You'll only get cranky instead of inspired. It takes time and energy to sort through the racks to find the perfect items.

Thrift a variety of material and gather other supplies before starting on your hacking projects.

Look carefully at clothing before buying it. If the lighting in the story is poor, walk over to a window so you can examine each **garment** for stains, rips, decorations, and tears. If you find problems, ask yourself if you can work around them. If not, put the clothes back on the rack.

Keep your eyes open for accessories you can use to improve your designs. The jewelry counter might have beads, buttons, pins, or chains that you could add to a denim bag. Suede or leather skirts can become handles, fringe, or patches. Belts make great bag straps.

As you shop, ask yourself: Can I make something great out of this? Is the price right? Does this item give me inspiration and great ideas? Is there enough fabric to work with? The projects in this book are just a jumping-off point for your imagination. Your own creations will be unique depending on the size, color, and personalization you choose to add. Let's get started!

Supplies Checklist

In addition to denim clothing, you will need the following items to complete the projects in this book:

- Sharp sewing scissors
- Chalk (You can use special dressmaker's chalk from the fabric store or regular blackboard chalk.)
- Very sharp straight pins (Long yellow quilting pins work great.)
- Ribbons, buttons, trim, and jewelry for decorating
- Polyester or poly-blend thread
- Ironing board, iron, and starch
- Tape measures
- Poly fiberfill **batting**

For sewing by machine:

- Extra-sharp sewing needles (labeled "denim")

For sewing by hand:

- Beeswax puck to coat thread before use
- Hand-sewing needles (labeled "sharps")
- Thimble to protect your finger when you push a needle through tough denim

For sewing-free creating:

- Fabric glue, iron-on **adhesive**, or double-stick fabric tape

Chapter 2

Hacking Denim Dresses

When you get to the thrift store, you might notice that a lot of the clothes for sale are unfashionable. Just look at all those long dresses from the '80s! Remember that you are buying things to hack, not things to wear as they are. Think of

It is easy to hack an old denim dress into a cape you can wear.

those dresses as a source of low-cost, durable fabric. Plus, many denim dresses are made of lightweight material, so they are easier to work with.

Let's start by creating a costume. Whether you're an actor, you're getting ready for Halloween, or you enjoy re-creating historical events, you need a cape. Best of all, almost no sewing is needed for this project!

Project 1: Cape

1. Clear off your kitchen table or a large space on the floor.

2. Lay a dress flat on the surface. Find the waist seam, where the skirt meets the **bodice** of the dress. Cut off the skirt just below the waist. If the dress doesn't have a waist seam, use a yardstick or tape measure to measure up from the bottom **hem** to about where the waist would be. Mark with chalk around the skirt. Connect the chalk marks until you have a line at the waist. Cut along the line. (The chalk line will come out in the wash.)

3. Some denim dresses have buttons down the center front of the skirt. If so, unbutton all of them so you now have a long rectangle of fabric.

If your skirt doesn't have buttons, cut off one side seam to open the skirt into a rectangle.

4. Ask a parent to help you iron out any wrinkles. Spraying the skirt with water or starch before ironing can help smooth out the wrinkles. You can also use the iron's steam feature.

5. Flip your fabric rectangle so the bottom hem is now at the top. Pinch the fabric on the inside of the hem and snip a slit with your scissors at each end. Be careful not to let the scissors go through both layers of fabric. Some dresses don't have hems wide enough for ribbon to fit through. If yours has a narrow hem, then instead fold the edge down 1.5 inches (3.8 centimeters) and stitch it down. (Fabric glue is not ideal for this project.)

6. Find a ribbon that is at least as long as the unfolded rectangle. Cut the ribbon's ends at an angle so they cannot **unravel**. Attach a safety pin to one ribbon end. Thread it through the bottom hem from slit to slit.

7. Now you're ready to wear your cape! Pull the ends of the ribbon and pin them together loosely around your neck.

8. If you like, cover your cape's bottom edge with ribbon, rickrack trim, or other decorative designs using fabric glue or stitches. You can also leave the edge raw and let it unravel over time. The unraveled edge might look cool on its own. (See laundering instructions in chapter four.)

Project 2: Puppet Stage

Whether you are entertaining your relatives or bringing a book report to life, a portable puppet stage is fun to have around. Create one using the bottom of a denim dress and a tension rod (a spring-filled curtain rod). Choose a rod wide enough to be installed in a doorway or narrow hallway. First, follow steps

Three Ways to Wear a Cape

1. **Vampire or Red Riding Hood:** Tie the cape firmly around your neck.
2. **Magician or superhero:** Drape the cape around your neck. Pull the ribbons in front of your armpits, then pull them behind you and have a friend tie the ends behind your back.
3. **Musketeer:** Drape the cape over one shoulder. Pull the front ribbon at an angle across your chest and the back ribbon across your back. Tie the ends together under your opposite armpit.

Once your curtain is done, put on a show for your friends and family.

1 through 4 for making a cape. Then continue with these instructions:

1.   Following the directions on the package, adjust the tension rod so it will fit snugly in your doorway or hallway.

2.   Insert the rod, instead of a ribbon, in the hem of the cape.

3.   Hang the rod in your doorway or hallway. Distribute the fabric evenly across the space.

Make sure the bottom of the fabric puddles just a little bit on the floor. Otherwise, people will see your feet when you perform! If the skirt is not tall enough to hide your puppeteers completely, make a second skirt and hang it above the first one. Break a leg!

More Quick Dress Hacks

Project 3: Map Your Village Put down a tarp on the floor, then lay your denim on top. Draw a path of roads, using chalk or masking tape to plan out your space. Now use acrylic or fabric paints to paint roads. Add trees, buildings, and more. Use a hair dryer to dry the paint quickly. Populate your village with toy cars, LEGO figures, and any other toys you have.

Project 4: Mural Lay your denim on a tarp and paint a work of art! Hang your creation on a wall using thumbtacks or pushpins.

Project 5: Hacked Top Take the leftover top from your dress and refashion it into a new shirt. Try wearing it backward! You can also use extra fabric to cut out shapes for small pillows or stuffed animals.

Chapter 3

Hacking Denim Jackets

Denim jackets have been the height of cool for a long time. When you thrift one, you can make it your own. We'll work on two **appliqué** projects in this chapter. *Appliqué* is a French word meaning "to add on." It's a fancy way of saying that we will add decorative patches to our clothing.

You can choose any emoji you want for the design on the back of your jacket.

Project 6: Fleece Emoji Patch

Emojis are tiny, cute pictures you can include in texts. Let's add one to the back of a jacket. We'll use fleece scraps for this project. Because this material won't unravel, you don't need to worry about raw edges when you wash it.

1. First, we need a pattern so we can trace our emoji's shape. Search online to find a picture of the emoji you want to use. Choose an image from the search results. Copy it and paste it into a slide show or word processing program.

2. Click and drag the corners of the emoji until it fills the screen.

3. Print it out in black and white. Don't worry if it looks fuzzy.

4. Cut out the main shape (probably a circle) using a pair of regular scissors. Don't use your sewing scissors. Cutting paper will dull the sharp blades. You need sharp scissors for cutting fleece!

5. Pin the shape to a corner of your fleece and cut around it with your sewing scissors. If it's awkward to cut around the pinned paper, trace it with chalk and cut along the chalk line.

6. Now cut out the mouth and eyes from the paper pattern. Use them to trace and cut pieces of fleece. If both eyes are the same, you can cut a single paper eye. Fold the fleece and cut both eyes out of the fabric at once.

7. Now you have all your pieces cut out. Use fabric glue to attach the eyes and mouth to the face. Use your face pattern to help place each item. If you think your jacket will get heavy-duty use, consider sewing in addition to gluing. If you do

Cut out the pieces of your emoji carefully so they will look good on your jacket.

Don't Iron Things Made from Milk Jugs!

Most fleece is made from recycled plastic, including milk jugs. This is great for the environment but bad for clothing irons. Keep fleece away from irons, or you will end up with a melted plastic mess!

You should sew or use fabric glue when you need to attach pieces of fleece to something. Never use iron-on adhesive with fleece!

this, apply the fabric glue only to the center of each piece so you don't have to stitch through it.

8. Let the glue dry.
9. Thread a needle and make small stitches around the edges of the eyes and mouth.
10. Now position the entire patch (face with eyes and mouth completed) on your jacket in the desired location.
11. Glue the face in the middle to hold it in place.
12. Let the glue dry.
13. Thread a needle and make small stitches around the edge of the face. Ta-da!

More Quick Jacket Hacks
Project 7: State-Shaped Appliqué Iron paper-backed fusible web (an iron-on glue) onto the back of colorful cotton or flannel fabric. Follow the instructions on the

package. Print out an outline of your home state to use as a pattern. Use the pattern to cut your state shape out of the fabric. Position your patch on your jacket and iron it on. If you have a sewing machine, zigzag stitch around the edges.

Project 8: Steampunk Vest Cut off the sleeves of a jacket. Decorate the vest with chains, gears from a take-apart project, or lace. Browse the hardware store for other interesting add-ons!

Project 9: Tie Art Arrange a thrifted men's tie artfully around the arm of a jacket. You could also place it across the jacket's front or back panel. Stitch or glue the tie down in an interesting shape.

Project 10: Re-Panel Showcase a special piece of fabric by gluing or stitching it to cover the back center panel of a jacket.

Project 11: T-Shirt Logo Cut the design from a worn-out favorite T-shirt and appliqué it to a jacket.

Project 12: Western Style Cut fringe from a thrifted suede skirt. Add it to your jacket's sleeves for a Western look. You can also cut designs from the suede and glue them onto the jacket's collar.

Project 13: Button Up Cover the bottom hem or cuffs of a jacket with dozens of buttons. Collect black or pearl buttons for a formal look or metal buttons to add military style.

Show some local pride by adding the outline of your home state to a jacket!

Chapter 4

Hacking Denim Pants

Jeans are the easiest clothing to thrift. You might spot ones that are pastel blue or deep midnight. They might be decorated with jewels or stitched patterns. They might be boot-cut or straight-leg. You'll find them all at your thrift store! The projects in this chapter can all be made using a single pair of straight-leg jeans.

Make sure you have heavy-duty pins and sewing needles before you start working with thicker jeans.

The denim used in pants is usually heavy-duty and tough to work with. Make sure you have sharp sewing scissors, denim-weight needles for your sewing machine, or "sharps" needles for hand-sewing. You can also use iron-on adhesive for many of these projects.

Project 14: Denim Storage Bag

Turn the leg of a pair of straight-leg jeans into a storage bag. The size of your finished project will depend on the size of your jeans and the amount you cut off the bottom of the jeans leg.

1. Roll the bottom cuff of a jeans leg. We folded the leg in our sample project (seen on the cover) twice. Determine how tall you want the finished bag to be. Measure this length down from the top of the cuff. For an 8-inch (20.3 cm) bag, measure down 8 inches (20.3 cm) from the fold line, then add about 2.5 inches (6.4 cm) for a total of 10.5 inches (26.7 cm). Measure at several points and mark the points with chalk. Connect the chalk points, then cut along the line.

2. Turn the leg inside out so you see the inside of the jeans leg. Bring the existing jeans seams

together so they almost match up in the middle, but adjust them so they don't overlap. This will make it easier to sew through the layers of denim.

3.   Use a sewing machine, a hand-sewing straight stitch, or iron-on hem tape to sew a seam 0.5 inches (1.3 cm) from the end of the material.

4.   Turn your bag right side out. Push in the bottom until the bag can stand up by itself.

5.   Glue on decorative ribbon or felt, or sew on buttons. You can also add decorative pins. Stuff your bag with goodies!

Project 15: Denim Mailbag

This is a quick variation on the Denim Storage Bag. Depending on the size of the jeans you use, you can turn this into a purse, a small book bag, an eyeglass case, or a costume piece.

1.   Start with a jeans leg that has not been previously cut. Fold over the hem about 5 to 7 inches (12.7 to 17.8 cm) so it makes a flap. Rub your chalk along the fold line so you remember where to fold it again after stitching.

2.   Now make a chalk line where you would like the bottom of your bag to be.

3.   Cut about 0.5 inches (1.3 cm) past the chalk line so you have enough fabric for the hem.

4.   Turn the leg inside out.

5.   Stitch the raw edge of the jeans leg closed. This seam will bear the weight of whatever you put in your mailbag. To make sure it is strong, make several rows of stitches or use two rows of iron-on hemming tape.

You can add patches or other decorations to personalize your bag.

6. Turn the bag right side out again. Refold the flap along your chalk line.

7. Add straps! Use some twill tape, woven belt material from the fabric store, or handles. Wrap them around your body the way you want to wear your bag. Pin the handles to your bag. Ask a friend for help if you can't reach.

8. Use hand-stitching or machine-stitching (iron-on tape or glue are less effective) to strongly secure the handles to just the back layer of denim. If you aren't careful, you'll sew your bag

Laundry Tips for Raw Denim Edges and Dye

Through wear and laundering, the threads and fibers on raw denim edges will rub against each other and unravel. This makes a fluffy-looking edge. You can hurry the unraveling process by making small fringe cuts along the raw edge, then tossing your project in with a few loads of laundry. But be careful. Denim is made out of big threads that can make a big mess in your washer as they come apart! To prevent this, place raw-edge denim in a pillowcase and tie it with a string before tossing it in the washer. Don't take the denim out of the bag until it is dry.

Denim also has **dye** that could come out the first few times it is washed. The dye could bleed into the washer water or rub into other fabrics. What a mess! Wash denim with similar colors and try a laundry cloth such as Shout Color Catcher. This will pull extra dye out of the water and prevent it from getting on other clothing.

shut! If you are using a sewing machine, put your bag on your sewing machine like a sock and make several rows of stitches. If you are hand-sewing, try sewing a rectangle first. Then make an X-shape in the center of the rectangle.

9. Decorate the flap with fringe, ribbon, pins, buttons, felt designs, or anything else you like.

Project 16: Autograph Pillow

In the 1950s, collecting autographs from friends, family, and celebrities was a hot hobby. Bring it back by creating a denim autograph pillow for your friend's next birthday!

1. Use chalk to draw a rectangle on a jeans leg.

2. Pin both layers of denim inside the rectangle so they can't move while you are cutting.

3. Cut out the rectangle. Make sure to cut through both layers of denim. If your scissors aren't sharp enough to cut both layers at once, cut the top layer and use it as a pattern to cut the bottom layer.

4. Stack the rectangle pieces on top of each other. Make sure the right sides are facing. This is a sewing term meaning that the outside of the

fabric pieces are facing inside the stack. The inside of the fabric should be showing on the outside of the stack.

5. Using stitches or adhesive hem tape, sew along both long edges and one short edge of the rectangles. Leave the fourth side free so you can put batting inside.

6. Turn your tube right side out. Use scissors to gently push out the corners until they look sharp.

7. Grab pieces of poly fiberfill batting about the size of an ice-cream scoop. Push them into the corners of your pillow case. If your fingers can't reach that deep, use the tip of your closed scissors to gently press the batting into the corners.

8. Keep adding small handfuls of batting until the pillow case is almost full.

9. Using your fingers and pins, fold over the open edges of denim to the inside. Pin the two edges shut. You shouldn't see any raw edge.

10. Use iron-on hem tape or stitches to close your pillow case.

11. Wrap up your pillow along with some markers as a gift for a friend. Sign your own name first!

More Quick Jeans Hacks
Project 17: Letter Pillow

Use chalk to draw a bubble-shaped letter on the leg of a pair of jeans. (You can also print out a big letter from your computer to make a pattern.) Make sure the letter is at least 2 inches (5.1 cm) wide at each point. Put pins through both layers to hold the denim in place. Cut about 0.5 inches (1.3 cm) outside of the chalk line. Stitch around the outline of the letter, but make sure to leave a space open so you can stuff it. Add batting (see tips on page 28) and stitch the letter closed.

Project 18 Seventies Beach Bag

Go retro! Cut off a pair of jeans above the crotch to make it look like a very short skirt. Turn it inside out and sew it closed along the bottom edge. Turn the bag right side out. Tie rope handles to the belt loops. Use the front and back jeans pockets for your sunglasses and sunscreen.

Congratulations, Fashion Hacker! You've tackled one of fashion's toughest fabrics and turned it into custom clothing, gifts, and toys. What will you try next?

Glossary

abundant (uh-BUHN-duhnt) plentiful or in great quantity

accessories (ak-SES-ur-eez) small items such as jewelry, belts, or bags that are worn with clothes

adhesive (ad-HEE-siv) a substance that makes things stick together

appliqué (ap-lee-KAY) a patch of fabric cut into a decorative shape and stitched onto another piece of fabric

batting (BAT-ing) a soft material used to stuff pillows, quilts, and other objects

bodice (BAH-dis) the top of a dress, from the shoulder to the waistline

dye (DYE) ink used to color fabric

garment (GAR-muhnt) an item of clothing

hem (HEM) an edge of material that has been folded and sewn down

landfills (LAND-filz) areas where garbage is piled and covered with soil

unravel (uhn-RAV-uhl) to become loose or pulled apart

Find Out More

BOOKS

Fontichiaro, Kristin. *Hacking Fashion: Fleece.* Ann Arbor, MI: Cherry Lake Publishing, 2016.

Fontichiaro, Kristin. *Hacking Fashion: T-Shirts.* Ann Arbor, MI: Cherry Lake Publishing, 2015.

WEB SITES

ReFashionista

http://refashionista.net

What if, every morning, you turned old clothes into your outfit for the day? ReFashionista Jillian Owens takes on this kind of challenge with her fun fashion projects.

The Renegade Seamstress

https://chicenvelopements.wordpress.com

What do teachers do after students go home? Kindergarten teacher Beth Huntington transforms into the Renegade Seamstress and refashions thrift store clothing! Follow her projects here.

Index

About the Author

Kristin Fontichiaro teaches at the University of Michigan. As head of the Michigan Makers and Making in Michigan Libraries projects, she helps kids and teens develop their maker creativity, and helps librarians and educators to launch and encourage hands-on maker learning in their communities.